*"Jacqueline takes you always directly to what you are ready to see or experience."*

— LONGTIME CLIENT AND READER

*"It is liberating to face your own blocks and to be finally free of the weight that they have caused for many years. And while for me the changes I'm experiencing are noticeable and real, I still feel like myself. Just a more sure self."*

— LONGTIME CLIENT AND READER

*"Jacqueline makes me BELIEVE I can be and live a joyful and magical existence every new day of my life!"*

— LONGTIME CLIENT AND READER

The *365 Days of Happiness* bestselling author

# JACQUELINE PIRTLE

# Of Course!

Because why wait...

A 30 day journal

# COPYRIGHT

I want to let you know that all my books and holistic practitioner work together, as a wholesome system, supporting you to live a more conscious, mindful, and happier life.

However, I made it so you can receive the benefit of living more joyously solely by working through this terrific journal book, while also experiencing the full satisfaction in continuing on to the next journal of this series—not to mention the rock solid tools you get by reading any of my other books or adding in my podcast *The Daily Freak*. Either way, I know you'll love my inspirational teachings.

Find out more at:
FreakyHealer.com
Amazon - Jacqueline Pirtle's Author Page
The Daily Freak Podcast

Before you dive in, I want to thank you for hopping on the magic train with me! I truly hope you enjoy *Of Course* as much as I loved writing it, and if you do, it would be wonderful if you could take a short minute and leave a review on Amazon and Goodreads.com as soon as you can.

Your kind feedback helps other readers find my books more easily, and to be happy faster. Consider it a joy-deed for the world.

Thank you!

# ACKNOWLEDGMENTS

Let's be honest here… I have a dream team!

I could not have finished this book without the help of talented, creative, high-for-life, and phenomenal professionals.

From the bottom of my heart, I want to thank Zoe Pirtle for her editorial mastery; Mitch Pirtle for his all-round support; kingwoodcreations.com for their fun and polished book cover design; and madiouART.com for an amazing photo shoot.

I'd also like to extend a huge "Thank You!" to all fans of my work and books—I created this beautiful journal series for you.

Life is spectacular with you on my side!

*Of course* your way through life and see what happens!

# DEDICATION

*I dedicate this journal to the words **of course**, and wish for them to brighten everything for everyone!*

# INTRODUCTION

Joyous *of courser*,

I am thrilled to show you how to *of course* yourself though your whole life, and present to you how cool and amazing your time here can actually be. Best of all, it will become unquestionably clear that you are in charge of how - and also what - your quality of existence is, and that you can change yourself to being and living more significantly at any time you wish.

The words *of course* have a legere - a but of course! - energetic attitude, but are also of a knowing and trusting character. Just think about it: "Of course I know what to do!" "Of course I am blessed!" "Of course this shall pass soon!" When thinking, saying, and writing *of course*, you shift into a nothing-is-that-serious-but-everything-is-a-given kind of frequency. There, a whole world of possibilities awaits you, because when relaxed, you are open and flexible and more of the unknown to the limited physical world can grab your attention—an attentiveness that is usually occupied by all physical life things.

This unknowingly and limitless wisdom comes from your energetic part—your soul being, your inner you, your higher self, however you wish to call it; and also from your one-ness with consciousness, a space where all information is held.

You are a whole being comprised of a physical body, mind, soul, and consciousness, here to experience life through physicality and alignment with your soul being—expanding and calibrating into *bigger and more* at all times through human-ness and from the core of the energetic essence that makes everything and everyone. As that energetic bundle, you are vibrating in frequencies - some being lower than others - with higher ones preferred since they are the ones that feel amazing. You are capable of switching between these frequencies as you wish. Simply said, what you focus on is how you feel and how you feel creates your next—it's like you are holding a compass and can constantly see where you are, but also where you are headed to:

- I am pointing upwards and heading higher—feeling great while latching onto even more blissfulness.
- I am focused downward and going into the abyss— feeling lower, and then even lower, while not doing any focused inner-work to uplift myself.

That is where the method of the powerful *of course* comes in handy, unless you were trained to and are practicing a rather unhelpful way of using *of course*. For example: of course I stub my toe, of course I'm getting sick right now, of course I did not get this job. Many times those downer ways are then followed by reasoning and explaining efforts - sometimes even "I knew this was going to happen" is added - unaware of the misuse.

This **Of Course** journal exists to set the low bar of expectations that you have to the height that you in your life deserve— helping you to turn your old ways upside down - and inside out - so nothing goes the old unhelpful way anymore. From there you can find new and unique preferences that fit your aligned being, so you will knowingly with sass and grace walk your high-for-life journey.

I say, let's change all misaligned *of course* usage into aligned of course-ing and use that power to create the life of your dreams—actually scratch that, make it a life beyond your dreams! There, an ocean of opportunities will catch hold of you—not to mention becoming ONE with bliss and the excitement of living an extraordinary life that is filled with incredible manifestations. Surely you understand that such a lifestyle still includes ups and downs and lefts and rights—lots of great material for you to practice of course-ing? I hope I hear a "Yes!" The trick is to successfully *of course* your way even through these times, and not give them the mighty downer momentum or wanting them to go away.

Journaling through this 30 day edition of **Of Course** gives your best version of you the spotlight and brings huge calibrations into the equation so you can experience life like you never have before, craft a time beyond your expectations, and love what you live—to the extent of becoming a master in living consciously, mindfully, and feeling phenomenal while manifesting the best of the best. It's a change that is forever!

As a side note, there are a couple of bonus days at the end in case you ever find the need to do two in a day, or so you can keep working while you wait for the next journal in this series to arrive. I also left you a few blank *of course* pages to journal about deepening your ways of being proudly alive.

Enough chit-chat, I know you are ready—so grab your pen and have incredible fun catching more life than you have ever caught in your new crazy ways.

Happiest,
   Jacqueline

ay 1

YOU ARE A DREAMER, and even if that is not your practiced every-day state, you have a dreamy side. Everyone does! So imagine that right now, you are that fantasizer, and are sitting on the most magical bench you have ever seen. You are breathing, relaxing, and smiling, because you know that you are about to shoot your heartfelt longings into the possible field of the universe. Dreamily, and with a hopeful gaze, you're looking up into the sky saying and thinking things like, "If I could just make things happen, have what I want, get a little help, and be happier, healthier, and more satisfied." "If it could just be a little bit better, more fitting, and with added blessings." "If they could just give me what I want, behave nicer, and be more positive." Go on, scribble all your *if I could-s, if it could-s,* and *if they could-s* down, then shoot them into the glory of consciousness—but make sure you are sitting on your dreamer bench first! How does it feel as that hopeful being, shooting desires up into the infinite sky? Are you soothed by releasing the burden of doing it all yourself? Is your heart lightening up by lessening the weight of carrying it all alone?

*Of Course - Because why wait...*

ay 2

GET your dreamer bottom onto that bench again—tune into your dreamy side and with an expectantly open heart look up into the sky, breathe, and maybe even close yours eyes to enjoy this pure moment. Then with playfulness and lightness say, "OK universe, yesterday I gave you all I got, what do you have for me?" To your surprise - but also matching your hopes - you hear, "Of course, it just so happens that I have a whole cosmos filled to the brim with your wishes and dreams, and to unlock, all you have to do is learn to *of course* your way through your journey." You ask, "How do I do that?" but sense right away from deep within your heart that this is a silly question because you already know the answer —through aligning with who you really are, steering your focus towards your dreams, and using the words *of course* to heighten your whole being and expectations into the frequency of these manifestations.

Go ahead, beautiful *of courser*, take your list from yesterday and rephrase your *if I could, if it could,* and *if they could* to *of course I can, of course it can,* and *of course they can*—or even better, *of course I AM, of course it IS,* and *of course they ARE*. How do you feel now?

_____

_____

_____

_____

_____

_____

*Of Course - Because why wait...*

ay 3

*OF COURSE CARRIES* an energy of knowledge, sureness, freedom, strength, and power, even being a magician of some sort because you are making the magic happen for yourself—that is, if you use *of course* in correct ways. Hence, there is a difference in saying "Of course this stupid thing happened to me," and "Of course I am the best and most beautiful person ever."

Saying, thinking, writing, and breathing into these words and their magical energetic value shifts you immediately into a frequency where everything is possible—a space that is actually and naturally how the world and life IS when humans don't mess with it through focusing on being scared, angry, negative, or when we behave powerless and believe that life is hard to endure.

How will you get your whole being into the trance of the *of course* magic and stay in this amazing world of possibilities?

_____

_____

_____

_____

_____

_____

_____

_____

_____

_____

_____

_____

_____

**Of Course - Because why wait...**

ay 4

An *of course* lifestyle means that you trust in yourself! It's a belief that you are supposed to be here, a knowing that you are worth it and deserve to live a marvelous life, and the craving for an excellent alignment and relationship with your inner being and the universe—to manifest and co-create, of course, your best life ever. How will you create and nourish your self-trust and stay focused on that solidness? Hint, hint, rehearsing, "Of course I live my best life ever!" is a great start!

_____
_____
_____
_____
_____
_____
_____
_____
_____
_____
_____
_____
_____
_____
_____
_____
_____
_____

*Of Course - Because why wait...*

ay 5

*OF COURSE LEAVES* nothing in question because it brings up the factual energy of "what else could it be," shifting you into a state in which it feels good to be full of yourself and sure about your life. How wonderful, to climb onto a higher pedestal than you were before since it's natural to ascend and align with your always expanding and calibrating inner you that constantly guides you to BE and live your best. Make "Of course!" be part of your daily vocabulary—make a solid *of course* usage list right now!

_____

_____

_____

_____

_____

_____

_____

_____

_____

_____

_____

_____

_____

_____

_____

_____

_____

*Of Course - Because why wait...*

ay 6

WHO COULD you shower with an *of course* attitude that goes something like this: "Of course life loves me!" As for the who, yourself—and who else? What *of course* expressions, actions, words, foods, drinks, clothing, and new choices or decisions can you come up with? This is an exercise of being sure of yourself and life—expect to have a great time while leaving no oxygen for stress, being powerless, or feeling limited. Go all *of course* here!

*Of Course - Because why wait...*

ay 7

USE the *of course* method for amazing health and energy by talking to, for, and about your body in a *my-health-is-a-given* sure way—creating millions of "how else could it be" moments that are filled with wholesome wellness. Great examples are: "Hey my gorgeous heart, of course you are happy, healthy, and strong!" or "Of course my feet are carrying me fast and swift through the jungle of my life—and might even climb for me if needed!" or "Of course I am losing weight and getting fit in the perfect way for me!" C'mon sure one, what are your powerful physical statements?

_____

_____

_____

_____

_____

_____

_____

_____

_____

_____

_____

_____

_____

_____

_____

*Of Course - Because why wait...*

ay 8

CONSCIOUSLY FILLING your mind with *of course* thoughts not only shifts your thinker-health into amazingness, it also changes your life since what you think can become your next physical NOW. Thoughts like, "Of course I'm fantastic," or "Of course I get this terrific new job," and "Of course all is well," changes the chemistry of every single cell of your whole being—your body, mind, soul, and consciousness. That means your output of energetic value changes to a higher level and what you experience in your outer world will shift to match your thinker-perfectness—since what is present in your surroundings mirrors what is in your inner core. Hence, of course life is rosy no matter the circumstances! To be ready and steady, what are some *of course* musings that get your smile going?

_____

_____

_____

_____

_____

_____

_____

_____

_____

_____

_____

_____

_____

*Of Course - Because why wait...*

ay 9

*OF COURSE* BRINGS an end to your waiting game, but not through the unhelpful energetic essence of "enough already," which creates resistance and pressure. No, it's through setting your expectations to trust, knowing, and feeling secure enough to invite the universe to deliver freely and happily. It's like the words *of course* wipe your desires clear and pure of everything that keeps your frustrating hurdles alive. *Of course* is intentional and has the calculated value of it IS. What waiting games are you holding onto—where do you want things to speed up and where are you holding yourself back? List every aspect of life—job, love, money, health. What of course-ing can you use to wipe all un-helpfulness away?

_____
_____
_____
_____
_____
_____
_____
_____
_____
_____
_____
_____
_____
_____
_____

*Of Course - Because why wait...*

ay 10

OF COURSE you are a soul being, an energetic essence of limitlessness, which is undoubtedly the biggest part of you—one that always IS and never goes. Aligning your whole being with that highest self is who you really are, and because of that, will always feel phenomenal to be in sync with. It's where your capability of expanding, calibrating, and then vibrating in the fitting frequency lies. But of course you know that already! How will you feel yourself into alignment and *of course* your way through your life more often?

_____
_____
_____
_____
_____
_____
_____
_____
_____
_____
_____
_____
_____
_____
_____
_____
_____
_____

*Of Course - Because why wait...*

ay 11

YESTERDAY WE HAD A SOUL-FULL CHAT, today let's wrap the rest...

Of course you have a physical body—one that allows your biggest part of you, your inner being, to park its grandness so you can experience physical life through it as long as your lifetime lasts! But you are also a consciousness, holding limitless information and connecting you to be ONE with everything. Highlighting that alignment in - but also as - your whole being is crucial. Living like you are consciousness and are being ONE with all immediately shoots you into the company of what the universe IS, and the bright offering it has in store for you—constant and 24/7 magic. How will you grab those wonders, and also use them?

_____

_____

_____

_____

_____

_____

_____

_____

_____

_____

_____

_____

_____

_____

_____

*Of Course - Because why wait...*

ay 12

WHEN IN DOUBT CHOOSE HAPPINESS! Why? Because the other option is to stay doubtful, which is way on the opposite end of being sure, knowing, and living your full capability to *of course* your way towards a beautiful NOW. Feeling blissful is on the same page as how-else-could-it-be and what-am-I-waiting-for, all while showing up as the aligned of-course-I-choose-a-marvelous-life energy that you naturally are. How will you choose happiness more often and how will you stay alert for when you are not in your *of course* ways?

_____

_____

_____

_____

_____

_____

_____

_____

_____

_____

_____

_____

_____

_____

_____

_____

_____

_____

*Of Course - Because why wait...*

 ay 13

IMAGINE a white canvas with nothing on it—that is how your new day looks with every fresh start! So get on your painter jumpsuit and artist beret, grab those colors and brushes, and be ready to creatively go crazy to paint the most unique and well-feeling art piece of the day. Start off like that every single morning—what is it going to be today? What colors, surroundings, clothing, moods, thoughts, foods, places, and what kind of people match your creation? Of course you got this—paint, *of courser*, paint!

_____
_____
_____
_____
_____
_____
_____
_____
_____
_____
_____
_____
_____
_____
_____
_____
_____
_____

*Of Course - Because why wait...*

ay 14

"OF COURSE I WANT THIS!" has immense power in setting the intention and expectation the way it needs to be in order for what you want to come your way. But there is more—breathing and feeling into the of courseness of the desired grounds the roots of what makes you happy deeply and securely. Add the visualization and imagination of these incredible dreams already being alive, and you have the perfectly successful cocktail for any manifestation to BE. What are you waiting for? Of course *DO* WANT A LOT!

_____
_____
_____
_____
_____
_____
_____
_____
_____
_____
_____
_____
_____
_____
_____
_____
_____
_____
_____

*Of Course - Because why wait...*

ay 15

WHAT ARE YOUR BIGGEST STRUGGLES? List them without getting all wrapped up in the why, what, and where—instead, do it robot like and without emotions. Have some fun here!

Next say, think, or write for every listing, "Of course I struggle with this because I don't want it this way!" or "Of course this is a goner because I don't like this trouble." or "Of course it's out the door because I deserve it to go ciao-ciao." or "Of course this stops right now because this trouble is not my jam." This gives you a clean slate - without negativing or going into detail - to move on and create differently.

Time to come up with your best case scenarios and use *of course* in manifesting ways through talking, thinking, and writing about your desired outcomes. What do you want it to be and what *of course* phrases fit those outcomes?

Reminder, always make it about yourself - no inclusion of others - and stay positive and humorous.

_____
_____
_____
_____
_____
_____
_____
_____
_____
_____

*Of Course - Because why wait...*

ay 16

OF COURSE SCREAMS CONFIDENCE—AS you, in you, and for you. Not to mention other people's googly-eyes when you - especially during your biggest life changes ever - say, "Of course this is right for me!" It shows trust in you living exactly what you are here to live so you can expand and calibrate into what you are here to BE, and if you are ever chasing after the alignment with confidence - because you feel timid - stop, easy-peasy say or think, "Of course I am courageous!" and automatically you will have reached the energetic value of confidence. Notice that *of course* really is a slam-dunk winner way of showing up.

_____
_____
_____
_____
_____
_____
_____
_____
_____
_____
_____
_____
_____
_____
_____
_____

**Of Course - Because why wait...**

ay 17

WHAT NEWNESS ARE you looking for? Is it a new job, a fresh passion, or a new and exciting vacation destination—new love, a baby, or a different adventure of maximum satisfaction? No matter the newness that you are looking for, what *of course* can you come up with to make its arrival a speedy event?

_____

_____

_____

_____

_____

_____

_____

_____

_____

_____

_____

_____

_____

_____

_____

_____

_____

_____

_____

_____

*Of Course - Because why wait...*

ay 18

HEAR YOURSELF SAY "OF COURSE!" and notice the sure, trusting, and huge energy you become when guaranteeing to yourself and the world that life brings you what you are asking for. Notice all the *of course*-es around you—birds taking off and, of course, landing just fine somewhere. Planes taking off and, of course, knowing their course. Books that, of course, entertain with their words. Of course-ing is everywhere—some might even say it is a normal part of life!

_____

_____

_____

_____

_____

_____

_____

_____

_____

_____

_____

_____

_____

_____

_____

_____

_____

_____

*Of Course - Because why wait...*

 ay 19

MAKE today the best *of course* day ever by carrying your of courseness wherever you go—walk like you mean it, dress like you wear it, act like you live it, and decide and choose like being it. You are a natural at being an *of course* creature, so own it! How will you do that?

_____
_____
_____
_____
_____
_____
_____
_____
_____
_____
_____
_____
_____
_____
_____
_____
_____
_____
_____
_____
_____
_____

*Of Course - Because why wait...*

ay 20

"OF COURSE I can have that, of course I am capable, of course my life is beautiful—of course, of course, of course!!!"

What unique power sentences can you come up with to make them your mantra—then say, think of, and act on at all times?

_____

_____

_____

_____

_____

_____

_____

_____

_____

_____

_____

_____

_____

_____

_____

_____

_____

_____

_____

_____

_____

_____

*Of Course - Because why wait...*

ay 21

THINK OF THE SKY, the sun and moon, the stars and clouds—the trees, flowers, ocean and rivers. If I ask you, "Are they naturally powerful, and are they always there?" you would laugh and say without any doubt, "Of course they are, silly you! Don't you see?"

That is the feeling we are looking for in this journal; that sureness and secureness, and that natural way of knowing and believing. How will you live your life more often being *that* sure about yourself and your existence?

_____

_____

_____

_____

_____

_____

_____

_____

_____

_____

_____

_____

_____

_____

_____

_____

_____

_____

*Of Course - Because why wait...*

ay 22

WHEN YOU SAY "OF COURSE!" it's natural to look upward or at least raise your chin—certainly never downward to the ground unless you are using it to certify something negative. You feel upward, carry yourself hopefully, and are filled with an extra amount of positivity, worth, pride, and satisfaction. How will you make sure that you notice this grandness in your new *of courser* life?

_____

_____

_____

_____

_____

_____

_____

_____

_____

_____

_____

_____

_____

_____

_____

_____

_____

_____

*Of Course - Because why wait...*

ay 23

I SAY, surprise others with synonyms for "Of course!"—just in case you need to spice things up, have more fun, or keep them from rolling their eyes at the *of course* person you have become. So here we go…

Definitely, certainly, obviously, undoubtedly, indeed, surely, without a doubt, indubitably, rainbowish-ly sure, unicorns never question anything, fairytales naturally happen for me, or magic is always around my corner. Which one is your new favorite go-to?

_____
_____
_____
_____
_____
_____
_____
_____
_____
_____
_____
_____
_____
_____
_____
_____
_____
_____
_____

*Of Course - Because why wait...*

 ay 24

WHEN YOU EAT BREAKFAST, lunch, dinner, and all the goodies in between, are those foods that you say *of course* to—or are you eating just to be eating? Do the sayings, "Of course this is delicious," "Of course this is nourishing," "Of course I want to eat exactly that," and "Of course there is nothing else I would rather be eating," resonate with your intake? If not, what food could you eat instead?

_____
_____
_____
_____
_____
_____
_____
_____
_____
_____
_____
_____
_____
_____
_____
_____
_____
_____
_____

*Of Course - Because why wait...*

ay 25

WHAT ARE you doing right now—besides enjoying this journal? Is it an *of course* activity? What is on your to-do list for today—lots of course-ing stuff? How can you put more weight onto filling your time with things that really matter to you? Particularly one that you enjoy, and that get your heart singing: "Of course I love my life!" Go on, list please!

_____

_____

_____

_____

_____

_____

_____

_____

_____

_____

_____

_____

_____

_____

_____

_____

_____

_____

_____

_____

_____

_____

*Of Course - Because why wait...*

ay 26

LIVING an *of course* lifestyle comes with sassiness, and to be honest, it's about time you get used to this terrific *it's good to be me* feeling—maybe even celebrate with a twirl while you're at it! What fresh daringness can you come up with, and how can you drench it with your best version of your *of course* you?

_____
_____
_____
_____
_____
_____
_____
_____
_____
_____
_____
_____
_____
_____
_____
_____
_____
_____
_____
_____
_____
_____
_____

*Of Course - Because why wait...*

 ay 27

IF YOU FEEL UNWELL, get scared, are sad, angry, frustrated, or if you loose hope, feel lost, and are devastated, it's easy to say, "Of course life is giving me lemons—of course everything is against me!" But such thoughts and feelings don't make sense, since there is never any aligned truth to them - soulfully and physically - and they certainly never feel good. Just think about it, your soul would never say "Of course you get the horrible stuff, being the weirdo that you are!" Where are you not aligning with your soul and, instead, are misusing the words *of course* in unhelpful ways?

_____
_____
_____
_____
_____
_____
_____
_____
_____
_____
_____
_____
_____
_____
_____
_____
_____
_____

*Of Course - Because why wait...*

 ay 28

Pick your most favorable treat—the one that, of course, will make you taste the most yummiest deliciousness. Do you doubt that treat, and its capability to send you into a magical state of ecstasy? Of course not! What are you waiting for? Grab that delicacy, and be aware of the shift into your high-for-life frequency.

_____

_____

_____

_____

_____

_____

_____

_____

_____

_____

_____

_____

_____

_____

_____

_____

_____

_____

_____

_____

*Of Course - Because why wait...*

ay 29

Do you ever feel like you can't breathe, are trapped, have no energy, are blocked, or something of that sort? The counter fight for these states is always to put your focus on the opposite and infuse your struggle with the power that *of course* carries. For example: Can't breathe—"of course my lungs are filled with plenty of oxygen." Trapped—"of course I am a free spirit." No energy—"of course my energy level is at its best." Blocked—"of course I am flowing nicely in every aspect of my being."

I say, *of course* yourself to the better case scenario at all times —however, if you need medical attention, of course go be seen!

*Of Course - Because why wait...*

ay 30

On an *of course* planet, in an *of course* universe, aligned with your *of course* inner you, how does your life look and how do you feel, think, act, and behave? Are you happy? Of course you are! Go all out and visualize your best of the best version of being and living you!

_____

_____

_____

_____

_____

_____

_____

_____

_____

_____

_____

_____

_____

_____

_____

_____

*Of Course - Because why wait...*

\* \* \*

READY TO CONTINUE on your self-growth path? Get the next journal in this series: ***Align, Expand, and Calibrate! Your Stairway to Joy***

# BONUS

*Because hey, no-one ever wants the goodness to end.*

*Of course, keep of course-ing!*

 ay 31

OF COURSE YOU ARE LIMITLESS!

How else could it be when the biggest part of you is an endless inner being filled with infinite wisdom, and your molecular essence is infinite energy that's changeable and full of possibilities? Add to these facts that the universe has your back and that you are ONE with consciousness, leaving all doubts to go poof, begone. You are truly a super power—of course you are!

_____

_____

_____

_____

_____

_____

_____

_____

_____

_____

_____

_____

_____

_____

_____

_____

_____

_____

_____

*Of Course - Because why wait...*

ay 32

YOUR HEART IS longing for you to say, think, dance, and feel that it is normal to use the grand love it produces to nourish the love you have for yourself—then, from that full tank of self-care, you are instructed to spread and share with everything and everyone. Your heart has another message: **Stay full of yourself, be true to yourself, and - of course - love yourself!** Not just for now, but **always**!

*Of Course - Because why wait...*

Day 33

TAKE your sweet time to practice becoming a genius *of courser!* But beware, I did not say "wait to become one." Because why wait when, all along, the only perfect time is NOW—and holding out for imaginary glimpses of better times is a hallucination, since you are the one that creates them? Go for it, spectacular *of courser*, you so got this!

_____

_____

_____

_____

_____

_____

_____

_____

_____

_____

_____

_____

_____

_____

_____

_____

_____

_____

_____

*Of Course - Because why wait...*

 ay 34

OF COURSE NAY-SAYERS, negative-ers, and down-ers exist, and at times everyone is one of those—even you and I! So how do you get yourself out of this space of nonsense-ness?

Of course, by going into the opposite of these low frequencies —instead of nay say yay, go from negativing to positiving, and heighten yourself when you are downing.

*Of course* yourself back in order, inspiring one, so others are invited to do the same. Onward and happy is the goal!

---

**Of Course - Because why wait...**

ay 35

HOW MANY TIMES can you infuse your personality, words, actions, and thoughts with "Of course!" today? 10 times—not enough! 100 times—you can do better! 1000 times; okay that's nice. How about a million times? I challenge you because, of course, why not!

*Of Course - Because why wait...*

AND NOW IT'S YOUR TURN!

*The following are your magical pages to become your own "what else could it be" of courser champion!*

*I'm counting on you to go all out here!*

ay 36

OF COURSE I...

_____
_____
_____
_____
_____
_____
_____
_____
_____
_____
_____
_____
_____
_____
_____
_____
_____
_____
_____
_____
_____
_____
_____
_____
_____
_____
_____
_____
_____

*Of Course - Because why wait...*

# Day 37

OF COURSE IT...

_____
_____
_____
_____
_____
_____
_____
_____
_____
_____
_____
_____
_____
_____
_____
_____
_____
_____
_____
_____
_____
_____
_____
_____
_____

*Of Course - Because why wait...*

ay 38

OF COURSE THEY...

*Of Course - Because why wait...*

ay 39

OF COURSE WE...

_____
_____
_____
_____
_____
_____
_____
_____
_____
_____
_____
_____
_____
_____
_____
_____
_____
_____
_____
_____
_____
_____
_____
_____
_____
_____

*Of Course - Because why wait...*

ay 40

OF COURSE...

_____
_____
_____
_____
_____
_____
_____
_____
_____
_____
_____
_____
_____
_____
_____
_____
_____
_____
_____
_____
_____

***Of Course - Because why wait...***

\* \* \*

Don't forget to leave a review on Amazon.com and
Goodreads.com as soon as you can, as your kind feedback helps
other readers find my books easier. Thank you!

*365 Days of Happiness*

*Because happiness is a piece of cake!*

This passage book invites you to create a daily habit to live your every day joy, and is the parent companion to *365 Days of Happiness*, the journal workbook.

\* \* \*

*365 Days of Happiness - Special Edition*

*Because happiness is a piece of cake*

This beautiful Special Edition of the bestseller *365 Days of Happiness: Because happiness is a piece of cake* has room for your notes after every daily passage.

\* \* \*

*365 Days of Happiness - Journal Workbook*

*Because happiness is a piece of cake*

This enlightening journal workbook is your daily tool to create a habit of living your every day bliss, and is the companion to *365 Days of Happiness: Because happiness is a piece of cake*.

\* \* \*

*Life IS Beautiful - Here's to New Beginnings*

If you like digging deeper into the meaning of life and are inspired by spirituality, then you'll love Jacqueline's effective teachings.

\* \* \*

*Parenting Through the Eyes of Lollipops*

*A Guide to Conscious Parenting*

If you like harmony at home and laughter in the house, then you'll love Jacqueline's inspirational methods.

\* \* \*

*What it Means to BE a Woman*

*And Yes! Women do Poop!*

If you like to live free, empowered, and want to decide for yourself, then you'll love Jacqueline's liberating ways.

\* \* \*

*Life-changing Journals*

*What. If. - Turning your IFs into it IS!*

*Open - Where it all starts!*

*To BE and Live - The reason you are here!*

*High for Life - The best case scenario!*

*Bragging - Because you're worth it!*

*Align, Expand, and Calibrate - Your Stairway to Joy*

Every journal comes in two lengths:

A 30 day journal

A 90 day journal - The Extended Edition

If you like being in charge of your own life, turning your dreams into reality, enjoy journaling, and want to squeeze the most out of your time, then you'll love Jacqueline's uplifting teachings.

# ABOUT THE AUTHOR

Bestselling author, podcaster, and holistic practitioner, Jacqueline Pirtle, has twenty-four years of experience helping thousands of clients discover their own happiness. Jacqueline is the owner of *FreakyHealer* and has shared her solid teachings through her podcast *The Daily Freak*, sessions, workshops, presentations, and books with clients all over the world. She holds international degrees in holistic health and natural living. Her effective healing work has been featured in print and online magazines, podcasts, radio shows, on TV, and in the documentary *The Overly Emotional Child by Learning Success*, available on Amazon Prime.

For any questions you might have, to sign up for Jacqueline's newsletter, and for more information on whatever else she is up to, visit www.freakyhealer.com and her social media accounts @freakyhealer.

Made in the USA
Middletown, DE
11 September 2021

48086312R10036